D1706476

STATE PROFILES

ARKANSAS

BY PATRICK PERISH

BELLWETHER MEDIA • MINNEAPOLIS, MN

Blastoff! Discovery launches a new mission: reading to learn. Filled with facts and features, each book offers you an exciting new world to explore!

BLASTOFF! UNIVERSE

BLASTOFF! Beginners — GRADE K

BLASTOFF! READERS — GRADES 1-3

BLASTOFF! DISCOVERY — GRADE 4

This edition first published in 2022 by Bellwether Media, Inc.

No part of this publication may be reproduced in whole or in part without written permission of the publisher.
For information regarding permission, write to Bellwether Media, Inc., Attention: Permissions Department,
6012 Blue Circle Drive, Minnetonka, MN 55343.

Library of Congress Cataloging-in-Publication Data

Names: Perish, Patrick, author.
Title: Arkansas / by Patrick Perish.
Description: Minneapolis, MN : Bellwether Media, Inc., 2022. |
   Series: Blastoff! Discovery: State profiles | Includes bibliographical
   references and index. | Audience: Ages 7-13 | Audience: Grades
   4-6 | Summary: "Engaging images accompany information about
   Arkansas. The combination of high-interest subject matter and
   narrative text is intended for students in grades 3 through 8"–
   Provided by publisher.
Identifiers: LCCN 2021019701 (print) | LCCN 2021019702 (ebook) |
   ISBN 9781644873755 (library binding) |
   ISBN 9781648341526 (ebook)
Subjects: LCSH: Arkansas–Juvenile literature.
Classification: LCC F411.3 .P47 2022 (print) | LCC F411.3 (ebook) |
   DDC 976.7–dc23
LC record available at https://lccn.loc.gov/2021019701
LC ebook record available at https://lccn.loc.gov/2021019702

Editor: Colleen Sexton   Designer: Andrea Schneider

Printed in the United States of America, North Mankato, MN.

TABLE OF CONTENTS

THE SPRINGS

The bubbling spring water in Hot Springs National Park has formed over thousands of years. Rainwater flows deep into the earth. It heats up and rises back to the surface through cracks in the earth's crust.

HOT SPRINGS NATIONAL PARK
HOT SPRINGS

A family arrives in the city of Hot Springs, nestled in the Ouachita Mountains. They are ready for a relaxing day at Hot Springs National Park. There, steam rises from pools in the hills. These calming waters have drawn people for hundreds of years. The family finds the historic bathhouses that line the park road. They are soon soaking in the soothing spring waters.

ARKANSAS POST MUSEUM

BLANCHARD SPRINGS CAVERNS

CRATER OF DIAMONDS STATE PARK

LAKE OUACHITA

Later, they take a hike along park trails. Wildflowers bloom under oak and pine trees. The winding path leads the family to Hot Springs Mountain Tower. A breathtaking view awaits them at the top. Welcome to Arkansas!

Arkansas is in the southern United States. It covers 53,179 square miles (137,733 square kilometers). Oklahoma borders Arkansas to the west. Missouri lies to the north. The Mississippi River forms Arkansas's eastern border with Tennessee and Mississippi. Louisiana is Arkansas's southern neighbor. The southwest corner reaches Texas.

Arkansas's capital city, Little Rock, sits in the center of the state. Fayetteville and Fort Smith are large cities in the northwest. This region is also part of the mountainous U.S. Interior Highlands. It contains Mount Magazine, Arkansas's highest point.

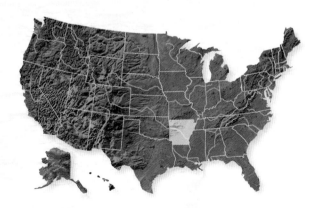

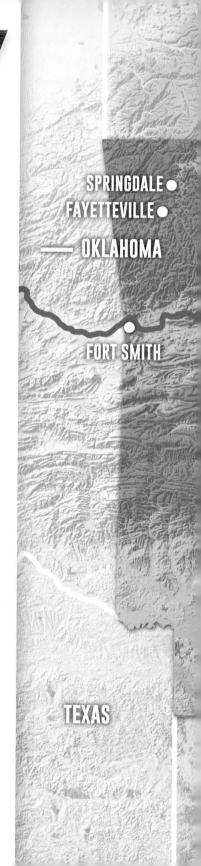

SPRINGDALE ●
FAYETTEVILLE ●
— OKLAHOMA

FORT SMITH

TEXAS

MISSOURI

N
W + E
S

JONESBORO

TENNESSEE ——

ARKANSAS
RIVER

ARKANSAS

LITTLE ROCK

HOT SPRINGS

MISSISSIPPI
RIVER

NAME IT!

Arkansas was the French name for the Quapaw people. It means "people of the south wind."

MISSISSIPPI

LOUISIANA

BATTLE OF ARKANSAS POST

ARKANSAS POST

In 1686, Arkansas Post was a trading center on the Arkansas and Mississippi Rivers. It became a thriving port that served as the Arkansas territory's first capital. Later, it was captured by the Union during the Civil War.

People arrived in Arkansas more than 10,000 years ago. In time, Native American groups formed. The Quapaw, Caddo, Osage, and other tribes lived in villages. They hunted animals and grew crops. Europeans first explored the area in 1541. **Settlers** began arriving in the late 1600s. They established large farms where **enslaved** Africans worked the fields.

The United States gained control of Arkansas after the **Louisiana Purchase** in 1803. The government soon began forcing Native American tribes off their lands to make room for settlers. Arkansas became the 25th state in 1836. It fought for the **Confederacy** in the **Civil War** from 1861 to 1865.

NATIVE PEOPLES OF ARKANSAS

There are no federally recognized tribes in Arkansas, though some Native Americans live in the state.

CADDO

- Original lands in Louisiana, Texas, Oklahoma, and Arkansas
- U.S. government pushed them into Oklahoma, where they now live

OSAGE

- Original lands reached from Missouri and eastern Kansas into northern Arkansas
- U.S. government moved them to Oklahoma, where they live today

QUAPAW

- Original lands in eastern Arkansas near the Mississippi and Arkansas Rivers
- U.S. government forced the tribe to Oklahoma, where it remains today
- Also called the Arkansas

The nickname the Natural State describes Arkansas well. Forests cover the northwestern highlands. Fast-flowing rivers weave between flat-topped ridges and **bluffs**. The Arkansas River Valley separates the Ozark and the Ouachita Mountains. Arkansas's southeastern half is flatter. The Delta region along the Mississippi River features swamps and a low **plain** with rich soil.

ARKANSAS RIVER

MISSISSIPPI RIVER —

N
W + E
S

☐ OZARK MOUNTAINS
■ OUACHITA MOUNTAINS

SWAMP
DELTA REGION

DIGGING FOR DIAMONDS

Arkansas is rich in minerals. Visitors can dig for diamonds at Crater of Diamonds State Park. The largest diamond found in the United States was discovered there in 1924!

ARKANSAS'S FUTURE: CLIMATE CHANGE

The effects of climate change are challenging Arkansans. Heavier rainfalls and increased flooding are occurring throughout the state. Droughts may also become more severe.

SPRING
HIGH: 72°F (22°C)
LOW: 52°F (11°C)

SUMMER
HIGH: 90°F (32°C)
LOW: 70°F (21°C)

FALL
HIGH: 73°F (23°C)
LOW: 53°F (12°C)

WINTER
HIGH: 52°F (11°C)
LOW: 34°F (1°C)

°F = degrees Fahrenheit
°C = degrees Celsius

Arkansas has a warm and **humid** climate. Winters are mild. Some snow falls, mostly in the highlands. Summers are hot. Tornadoes and severe storms sometimes sweep through the state. Flooding is common along river valleys.

Arkansas is home to amazing wildlife. Black bears search for nuts in oak and hickory forests while bats swoop through the air. Hungry bobcats stalk rabbits while raccoons paw across the forest floor. Minks find wooded homes near water. Along the Buffalo River, elk herds graze among columbine flowers. White-tailed deer and wild hogs roam the valleys and fields. Alligators rest in waterways near Arkansas Post.

Arkansas is a land of birdsong. No singer is more vocal than the mockingbird. In fall, thousands of **migrating** birds fly through Arkansas as they follow the Mississippi River south. They include mallard ducks and indigo buntings.

BLACK BEAR

BOBCAT

WHITE-TAILED DEER

ALLIGATOR

INDIGO BUNTING

OZARK
BIG-EARED BAT

Life Span: up to 15 years
Status: federally endangered

Ozark big-eared
bat range =

LEAST CONCERN	NEAR THREATENED	VULNERABLE	ENDANGERED	CRITICALLY ENDANGERED	EXTINCT IN THE WILD	EXTINCT

More than 3 million people call Arkansas home. About three out of five Arkansans live in Little Rock and other **urban** areas. Early settlers had **ancestors** from England, Ireland, and Germany. Some brought enslaved Africans. Polish, Jewish, Greek, and Italian families arrived throughout the 1800s and 1900s.

FAYETTEVILLE

FAMOUS ARKANSAN

Name: Johnny Cash
Born: February 26, 1932
Died: September 12, 2003
Hometown: Dyess, Arkansas
Famous For: An award-winning singer and songwriter whose music mixed country, rock, blues, and gospel styles

Today, most Arkansans have European ancestry. Over 1 in 10 Arkansans are African American or Black. Many Vietnamese and Laotian people arrived after the Vietnam War ended in 1975. Farming jobs drew many Hispanic **immigrants**. Springdale is home to a large Marshall Islander community. Small numbers of Native Americans still live in Arkansas.

Little Rock is the capital of Arkansas. It sits on the Arkansas River near the Ouachita Mountain foothills. The city became the capital of the Arkansas **Territory** in 1821. River access and railways made Little Rock an early trade center. Today, it is an important financial and retail city.

ARKANSAS RIVER

Little Rock is also a regional center of **culture** and entertainment. The Arkansas Arts Center features paintings, sculptures, and theater. The Museum of Discovery dazzles visitors with live science experiments. Community events showcase the city's **diverse** roots. The Jewish Food and Cultural Festival and the Greek Food Festival bring people together.

TESTAMENT: THE LITTLE ROCK NINE MONUMENT
LITTLE ROCK

THE LITTLE ROCK NINE

In 1957, U.S. troops protected nine students as they entered a Little Rock high school. The students were the first African Americans to attend an all-white school. The students became known as the Little Rock Nine.

Arkansas's key industries have helped shape the state. **Agriculture** continues to be strong today. Cotton, rice, soybeans, and wheat are top crops. Arkansas is a leading state for poultry production. The Tyson Foods headquarters is in Springdale. It is one of the largest meat-processing companies in the world.

ARKANSAS'S FUTURE: EDUCATION

Arkansas ranks low in quality of education and people with college degrees. Well-educated people often have skills that help a state's economy grow. They are also higher earners who pay more taxes. Improving education can help Arkansas's future economic success.

Arkansas is rich in **natural resources**. Forest workers cut down timber to make paper products. Miners take natural gas and oil from the ground. Factory workers make car and aircraft parts. Most Arkansans have **service jobs**. They work in hospitals, restaurants, and stores. The retail giant Walmart is headquartered in Bentonville.

INVENTED IN ARKANSAS

SYNCHRONIZED SOUND AND FILM

Date Invented: 1923
Inventor: Freeman Owens

WONDER HORSE

Date Invented: 1939
Inventor: William Baltz

KLIPSCH SPEAKERS

Date Invented: 1946
Inventor: Paul Klipsch

FRIED DILL PICKLES

Date Invented: 1963
Inventor: Bernell Austin

FOOD

BARBECUED PORK

Arkansans' favorite foods reflect Southern **traditions**. Breakfast often features cheesy grits or rice with sugar and butter. Cooks serve up barbecued pork with collard greens and black-eyed peas. Arkansas is famous for its fried foods. Fried chicken has always been popular. Fried pickles, okra, and green tomatoes are crispy and mouthwatering.

A WILD MEAL

Raccoon is on the menu in Gillett! The town's annual Coon Supper is a scholarship fundraiser.

Cheese dip is an Arkansas original. Arkansans eat it with tortilla chips, fries, and more! Mexican and African American traditions combine in spicy Delta hot tamales. Residents seek them out at roadside stands. For a sweet treat, Arkansans pour chocolate gravy over biscuits.

CHEESE DIP

CHOCOLATE GRAVY OVER BISCUITS

CHEESY BAKED GRITS

4 SERVINGS

Have an adult help you make these tasty grits!

INGREDIENTS

1 quart milk

1/2 cup and 1/3 cup butter

1 cup uncooked grits

1 teaspoon salt

1/2 teaspoon white pepper

1 cup shredded cheddar cheese

1/2 cup grated Parmesan cheese

DIRECTIONS

1. Preheat the oven to 350 degrees Fahrenheit (177 degrees Celsius). Lightly grease a medium baking dish.

2. Bring the milk to a boil in a pot over medium heat. Melt the 1/2 cup of butter in the boiling milk.

3. Gradually mix in the grits and cook for 5 minutes, stirring constantly.

4. Remove from heat and season with salt and pepper.

5. Beat with a whisk or electric mixer until smooth. Mix in the cheddar cheese and 1/3 cup of butter.

6. Pour the grits mixture into the prepared baking dish and sprinkle with Parmesan cheese.

7. Bake for one hour until firm.

SPORTS AND ENTERTAINMENT

KAYAKING

Arkansans enjoy the great outdoors. The many scenic trails draw hikers and mountain bikers. Wild rivers are great for floating or kayaking. Plentiful game makes hunting and fishing popular pastimes. Many Arkansans play or watch sports. Baseball fans love to catch an Arkansas Travelers game. Teams from the University of Arkansas also have a huge following.

SOOIE!

The University of Arkansas's mascot is the razorback, or wild hog. Fans have a unique chant. They shout "Whoo, Pig! Sooie!" to "call the Hogs."

A bustling arts scene is alive in Arkansas. The Crystal Bridges Museum boasts a stunning collection of American art. Folk, blues, and gospel music have a long history in the state. Live music shows draw audiences throughout Arkansas.

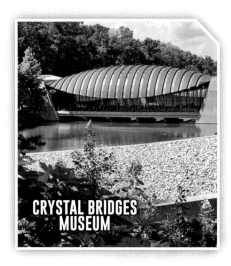

CRYSTAL BRIDGES MUSEUM

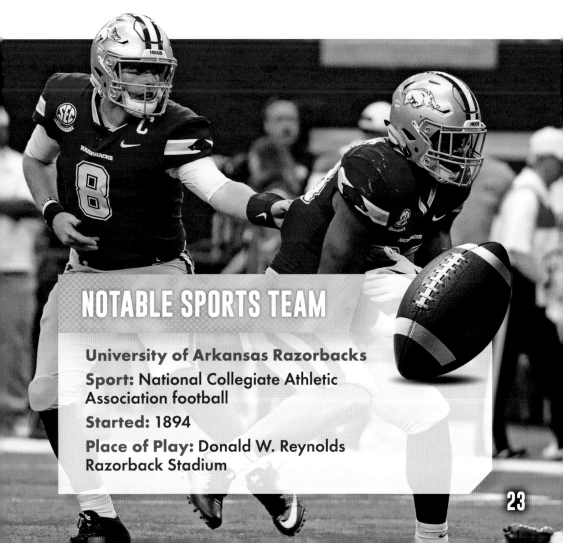

NOTABLE SPORTS TEAM

University of Arkansas Razorbacks

Sport: National Collegiate Athletic Association football

Started: 1894

Place of Play: Donald W. Reynolds Razorback Stadium

Arkansans have a lot to celebrate. Many festivals center on food, such as May's Picklefest in Atkins. The Hope Watermelon Festival in August also draws large crowds. Arkansans gather every October for the Arkansas State Fair. The celebration features farming exhibits, rides, and concerts.

Other traditions connect visitors to the past. Fans at the Rodeo of the Ozarks in Springdale watch riding and roping contests. The Ozark Folk Center preserves folk traditions. It offers live performances and workshops that showcase traditional mountain music. Visitors can learn quilting and other crafts. There is something for everyone in Arkansas!

TOAD SUCK DAZE

Local festivals often have strange names. Toad Suck Daze may be one of the strangest! Thousands of people head to Conway for the festival's live music, great food, and toad races!

24

OZARK FOLK CENTER

25

1541

Hernando de Soto leads the first European expedition into what is now Arkansas

1808

The U.S. government makes the first of several treaties forcing Native Americans to give up their lands

1836

Arkansas joins the Union as the 25th state

1686

Arkansas Post is the first European settlement built in Arkansas

1803

The Louisiana Purchase makes Arkansas part of the United States

1932

Arkansan Hattie Caraway becomes the first woman elected to serve a full term as U.S. Senator

1992

Former Arkansas governor Bill Clinton is elected president of the United States

1957

President Dwight Eisenhower sends U.S. troops to protect the Little Rock Nine

2018

Frank Scott, Jr. becomes the first African American to be elected mayor of Little Rock

1861

Arkansas fights in the Civil War for the Confederacy from 1861 to 1865

27

Nicknames: The Natural State, The Land of Opportunity

Motto: *Regnat Populus* (The People Rule)

Date of Statehood: June 15, 1836 (the 25th state)

Capital City: Little Rock ★

Other Major Cities: Fort Smith, Fayetteville, Springdale, Jonesboro

Area: 53,179 square miles (137,733 square kilometers); Arkansas is the 29th largest state.

Population
3,011,524
(2020)

STATE FLAG

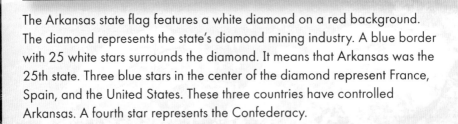

The Arkansas state flag features a white diamond on a red background. The diamond represents the state's diamond mining industry. A blue border with 25 white stars surrounds the diamond. It means that Arkansas was the 25th state. Three blue stars in the center of the diamond represent France, Spain, and the United States. These three countries have controlled Arkansas. A fourth star represents the Confederacy.

INDUSTRY

Main Exports

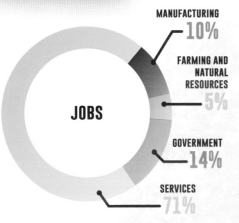

- MANUFACTURING
  10%
- FARMING AND NATURAL RESOURCES
  5%
- GOVERNMENT
  14%
- SERVICES
  71%

JOBS

poultry products

rice

aircraft parts

paper products

cotton

Natural Resources

timber, natural gas, oil, coal, bromine, stone, clay

GOVERNMENT

Federal Government

4 REPRESENTATIVES | **2** SENATORS

AR

6 ELECTORAL VOTES

USA

State Government

100 REPRESENTATIVES | **35** SENATORS

STATE SYMBOLS

STATE BIRD
NORTHERN MOCKINGBIRD

STATE ANIMAL
WHITE-TAILED DEER

STATE FLOWER
APPLE BLOSSOM

STATE TREE
PINE

agriculture—the practice of raising crops and animals

ancestors—relatives who lived long ago

bluffs—steep cliffs that often overlook a body of water

Civil War—a war between the Northern (Union) and Southern (Confederate) states that lasted from 1861 to 1865

Confederacy—the group of Southern states that formed a new country in the early 1860s; they fought against the Northern states during the Civil War.

culture—the beliefs, arts, and ways of life in a place or society

diverse—made up of people or things that are different from one another

enslaved—to be considered property and forced to work for no pay

humid—having a lot of moisture in the air

immigrants—people who move to a new country

Louisiana Purchase—a deal made between France and the United States; it gave the United States 828,000 square miles (2,144,510 square kilometers) of land west of the Mississippi River.

migrating—traveling from one place to another, often with the seasons

natural resources—materials in the earth that are taken out and used to make products or fuel

plain—a large area of flat land

service jobs—jobs that perform tasks for people or businesses

settlers—people who move to live in a new, undeveloped region

territory—an area of land under the control of a government; territories in the United States are considered part of the country but do not have power in the government.

traditions—customs, ideas, or beliefs handed down from one generation to the next

urban—related to cities and city life

TO LEARN MORE

AT THE LIBRARY

Gitlin, Martin. *Arkansas*. New York, N.Y.: Children's Press, 2019.

Kirchner, Jason. *Arkansas*. North Mankato, Minn.: Capstone Press, 2017.

Mooney, Carla. *The Little Rock Nine*. Minneapolis, Minn.: Abdo Publishing, 2016.

ON THE WEB

FACTSURFER

Factsurfer.com gives you a safe, fun way to find more information.

1. Go to www.factsurfer.com.

2. Enter "Arkansas" into the search box and click Q.

3. Select your book cover to see a list of related content.

INDEX